I0558485

ISBN 978-1-998317-85-1

Cover illustration and design by Charlotte Chang with the aid of artificial intelligence.

First Edition: April, 2025

1

很久以前，在古老的荒野中，有一座大山。
大山深处住着一群巨人，首领叫夸父。
夸父力大无穷，喜欢在耳朵上和手上挂着两条黄蛇。

Long ago, in the wilds of the ancient world, a giant mountain rose into the clouds. Deep inside lived a tribe of giants, led by their mighty chief, Kuafu. Kuafu wore two yellow snakes on his ears and often swung two more in his hands.

2

那时候的大地荒凉，常有猛兽出没山林。
夸父常带着族人去打怪兽。他勇敢又强壮，
大家都很信任和敬爱他。

Back then, the land was wild, and fierce beasts roamed the mountains. Kuafu often led his people to fight the monsters. He was brave and strong, and everyone trusted and loved him.

3

4

5

那年夏天特别热，太阳高挂天空，晒干了田地，烤枯了大树，山里连一滴水也没有了。夸父看到族人受苦，心里很难过，整天望着太阳发呆，想着办法。

That summer was hotter than ever. The sun stayed in the sky for a long time, burning the fields, drying the trees, and leaving the mountains without a drop of water. Kuafu felt very sad when he saw his people suffering, and he spent all day staring at the sun, thinking hard.

6

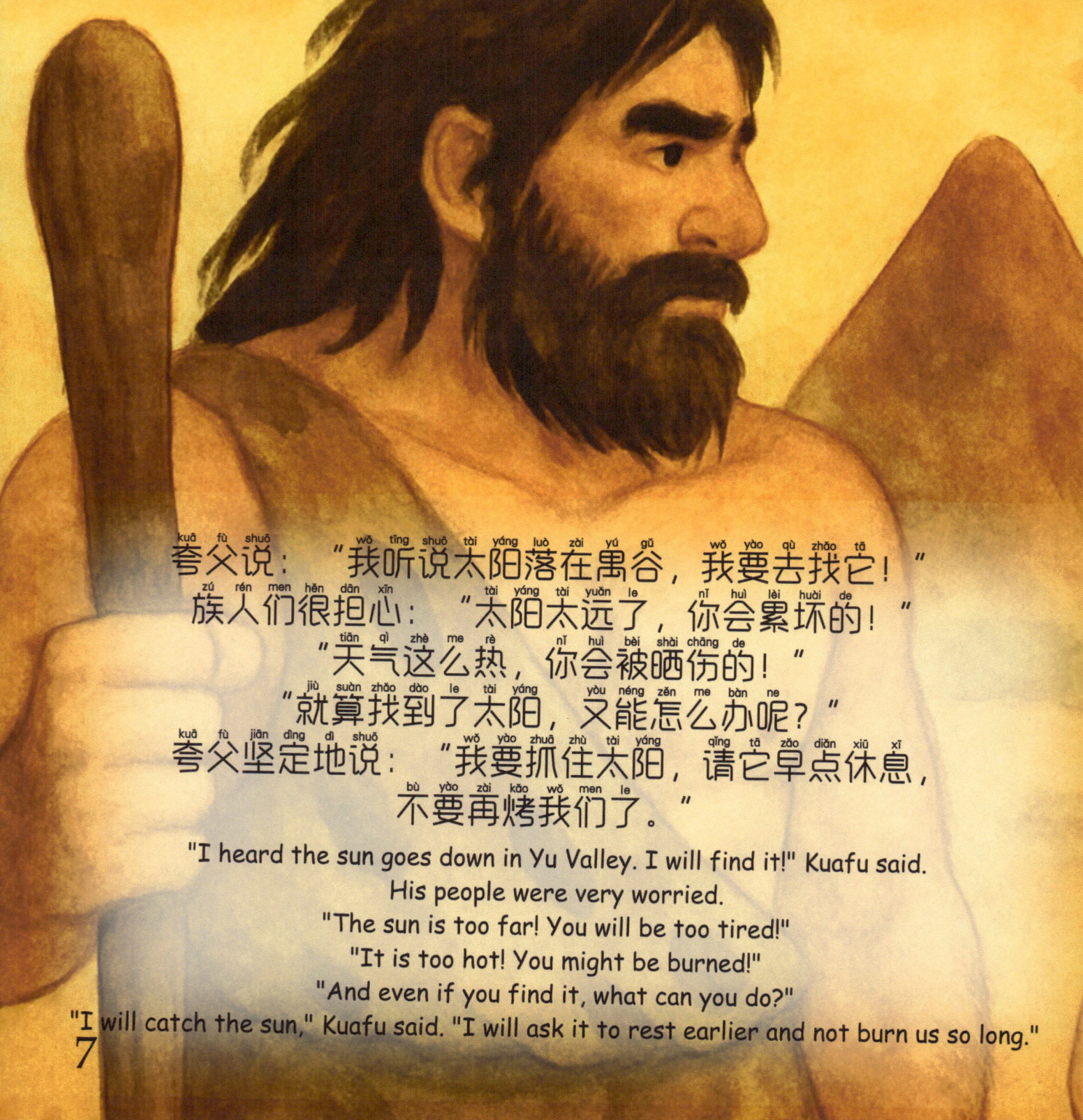

夸父说：“我听说太阳落在禺谷，我要去找它！”
族人们很担心：“太阳太远了，你会累坏的！”
“天气这么热，你会被晒伤的！”
“就算找到了太阳，又能怎么办呢？”
夸父坚定地说：“我要抓住太阳，请它早点休息，
不要再烤我们了。”

"I heard the sun goes down in Yu Valley. I will find it!" Kuafu said.
His people were very worried.
"The sun is too far! You will be too tired!"
"It is too hot! You might be burned!"
"And even if you find it, what can you do?"
"I will catch the sun," Kuafu said. "I will ask it to rest earlier and not burn us so long."

7

8

9

一天早上，太阳升起时，夸父向族人告别。
带着心中的梦想，他朝着太阳升起的东海方向，
踏上了漫长的追日之路。

One morning, as the sun rose, Kuafu said goodbye to his people.
With a big dream in his heart, he turned toward the East Sea, where the
sun came up, and began his long journey to chase it.

10

夸父翻过高山，跨过大河，跑过深谷，全力追赶太阳。
他跑得飞快，像是被风托着，脚一落地，大地都在震动

Kuafu climbed over tall mountains, crossed wide rivers, and ran through deep valleys. He chased the sun with all his strength. His feet moved so fast it felt like the wind was carrying him, and the ground shook with every step he took.

11

12

夸父口渴了，就捧起河水大口喝；肚子饿了，就摘野果充饥。他跑啊跑，鞋上的泥土掉了一地，堆成了一座座小土丘。

When Kuafu got thirsty, he scooped up river water and drank big gulps.
When he got hungry, he picked wild fruits to fill his belly.
He ran so far and for so long that the dirt falling from his shoes piled up into little hills on the ground.

13

15

夸父一直跑着，从不放弃，离太阳越来越近。终于，他感觉自己就要追到了。那颗又大又烫的红球就在眼前，周围洒满了金色的光芒。

Kuafu kept running, never giving up. He got closer and closer to the sun. At last, he felt he could almost catch it. The big, burning red ball was right in front of him, shining golden light all around.

16

太阳太热了，夸父口渴得不得了。
他喝光了一条小河，又喝干了黄河和渭河，还是很渴。

The sun was too hot. Kuafu was so thirsty that he drank up a whole small river, but he still felt dry. He ran to the Yellow River and drank it dry too, but it wasn't enough. Then he ran to the Wei River and drank it all, yet he was still very thirsty.

17

18

夸父又累又渴，差点摔倒，但他还在坚持。
"快到了，"他想，"前面有大沼泽，可以喝水。"
他想着那片水鸟嬉戏的大水塘。

Kuafu grew more tired and thirsty. He almost fell, but he kept going.
"I'm close," he thought. " I can find the big marsh and drink water there."
He dreamed of the wide waters where birds rested and played.

19

20

但夸父实在太累、太渴了。还没到沼泽，他就倒在地上，再也爬不起来。他用最后的力气，把手里的木杖用力地掷了出去。

But Kuafu was too tired and too thirsty. Before he could reach the marsh, he fell to the ground and could not get up again. With his last bit of strength, he threw his wooden staff as far as he could.

22

夸父的木杖落下的地方，长出了一片结满了甜美的果实的桃林。天帝被感动了，让太阳按时升起落下，夸父的族人也得救了。

从此，追赶太阳的夸父，成了人们永远传唱的英雄。

Where Kuafu's staff fell, a forest of peach trees grew, heavy with sweet fruit. The Heavenly Emperor was moved and made the sun rise and set at the right time. Kuafu's people were saved.

And so, the story of the giant who chased the sun was never forgotten.

23

24